INFLUENCES

By Bazzel Baz

Illustrations By Ken Dutton

Published by Pen, Cloak, & Dagger Inc.
California
United States of America

eBook ISBN 978-1-949280-11-1
Paperback ISBN 978-1-949280-10-4
Hardback ISBN 978-1-949280-09-8

Printed in the United States

There once was a man who came from a very dark and cold existence, a place where addictions and bad influences held him down from ever bettering himself, ever reaching a brighter future and happier days…a virtual sea of despair where he was drowning in a nightmare of compromise.

But one day he found the strength to break away from the evil influences and climb the steep cliffs of time and opposition. It certainly wasn't easy, and when he would look down at what he left below, it was downright scary.

With the grace of Almighty God and some perseverance he finally reached the top where things were not so tumultuous, life was full of sunshine, less stress and a promise for the future. He was on top of the world, so to speak, where confidence permeated his entire being.

And so he drew a line in the dirt as a reminder to never get too close to the edge of the cliff where he might fall back in. This became his mark of discipline…the standard he set for himself.

But from time to time he would sneak back to the line and maybe even cross the line to look over the edge of the cliff as if to kick up his adrenaline, push the envelope to excite himself or even just to remind himself of what his old life was like. And the more he would do this the more he found himself starting to enjoy this flirtatious tryst with the edge of the cliff. And soon the familiarity of his old life was temping him to jump back in.

But then…he came to his senses and stepped back to the other safe side of the line he had put in place for himself.

And so his life was pretty amazing until he invited some old influences in. Some of those were bad addictions from his past. They came in all forms and outnumbered him.

Some came in the form of food. Some came in the form of drugs. Some came in the form of stealing and lying and depression and narcissism and ego and

greed and pornography and entitlement.
And the list went on and on to every
influence he could think about that he had
previously left in the sea of despair below.

So all the bad influences he invited in began to crowd his life, began to take over and push him closer and closer to the very

dangerous edge of the cliff, beyond the line he had drawn for himself…crushing what discipline he had achieved.

He was not strong enough to fight back against the overwhelming crowd of influences, and they pushed him right over the edge of the cliff.

He was doomed to the sea of despair. And who would know, once he had fallen in, if he had what it would take to climb out again. And even if he did, he would be fighting on two sides…the bad influences in the sea of despair and the bad influences waiting for him at the top of the cliff.

That would take a lot of energy and frankly, did not sound like much fun at all. But better to climb and face the enemy than die in the sea of despair. And that is exactly what he did.

As he climbed he was sure that the bad influences would be waiting at the top, so he prepared himself for battle. He climbed with the determination to cast all of those bad influences over the side, off of the cliff.

And once he did, he stepped back on the other side of the line and got on with his life enjoying brighter and more stress-free days of happiness.

But one influence remained, one the man did not believe was of any danger to him…curiosity. As he recalled, it was never abrupt or pushy like the others and was rather benign in his own mind.

And so curiosity carefully and slowly began speaking to the man about the notion of peeping over the edge. The man began to move across the line out of curiosity and suddenly stopped. Suddenly he came to his senses, listening to a still, small voice deep inside him and realizing that if he did so, two things could happen.

Waiting just underneath the edge of the cliff could be those bad influences ready to grab him — the ones that may have been hanging on, some he may have been hanging on to — wanting to pull him back over the cliff's edge.

And even if the bad influences were not able to pull him over, even if he was stronger than before, the weight of the bad influences holding on and the struggle to get them to let go might in fact cause the entire edge of the cliff to give way from underneath him, causing him to plummet back into the sea of despair with all of them.

The man turned to curiosity and tossed it over the edge of the cliff. He sat back finally understanding enough about himself to realize the only way he was going to enjoy a happy life was to adhere to good discipline and stay on the right safe side of the line he had drawn for himself and to never, ever again invite bad influences in.

The end.